BASKETBALL
MATH ON THE COURT

—BY TOM ROBINSON

Published by The Child's World®
1980 Lookout Drive • Mankato, MN 56003-1705
800-599-READ • www.childsworld.com

Acknowledgments
The Child's World®: Mary Berendes, Publishing Director
The Design Lab: Design and production
Red Line Editorial: Editorial direction

Photographs ©: Sue Ogrocki/AP Images, Cover; Alonzo
Adams/AP Images, 4; Gheorghe Roman/Shutterstock
Images, 6–7; Jack Dempsey/AP Images, 8–9; Mark
Humphrey/AP Images, 10; David Hood/AP Images, 13;
Domenic Gareri/Shutterstock Images, 14; Shutterstock
Images, 17; Paul Vathis/AP Images, 18; Richard Paul
Kane/Shutterstock Images, 20; Christopher Penler/
Shutterstock Images, 21; Aspen Photo/Shutterstock
Images, 22–23, 29; Mark J. Terrill/AP Images, 25; Jeff
Tuttle/AP Images, 27

ISBN 9781614734086
LCCN 2012946503

Printed in the United States of America
Mankato, MN
November, 2012
PA02144

ABOUT THE AUTHOR

Tom Robinson is the author of 33 books, including 25 about sports. The Susquehanna, Pennsylvania, native is an award-winning sportswriter and former newspaper sports editor.

TABLE OF CONTENTS

Oklahoma City Thunder forward Kevin Durant (35) shoots a three-pointer to win the game against the Dallas Mavericks on December 29, 2011.

MATH ON THE COURT

The Oklahoma City Thunder has a timeout. There is one second left. It is early in the 2011–12 National Basketball Association (NBA) season. The Dallas Mavericks lead the game 102–101. The Thunder has time for one shot. Thabo Sefalosha finds Kevin Durant with a pass. The clock starts. Durant only has time to catch and shoot. Positioned 28 feet away from the basket, that is what Durant does. Durant sinks the shot. The Thunder wins. The crowd at the Chesapeake Energy Arena goes wild.

It's fun and fast-paced on the court. And a lot of math is needed to play the game and keep score. Numbers are used in many ways. There are different measurements. Time is counted down. The shots earn points. Durant knows how to get the ball to the rim that is 10 feet high. Teams can score one, two, or three points at a time. Math is involved as the points pile up. Coaches, TV announcers, writers, and fans use **statistics** to explain a game or season.

Use your math skills as you take a look at basketball. You'll be surprised at how much they are needed!

THE BASICS

The Court

Courts need to be measured and marked. Most have the same measurements, but some are different. Youth league courts are different from college courts. Courts in some countries are a different size than those in the United States.

To make a shot, the ball needs to go up a certain distance. The rim is 10 feet above the floor on most basketball courts.

The foul line is 15 feet from the face of the backboard. Lines are made to mark three-point shots. They start at 19.9 feet in high school. They extend as far as 23.6 feet for the NBA. The lane width and shape also changes. The foul line is an example of an international change. International foul lines are 15.1 feet from the backboard.

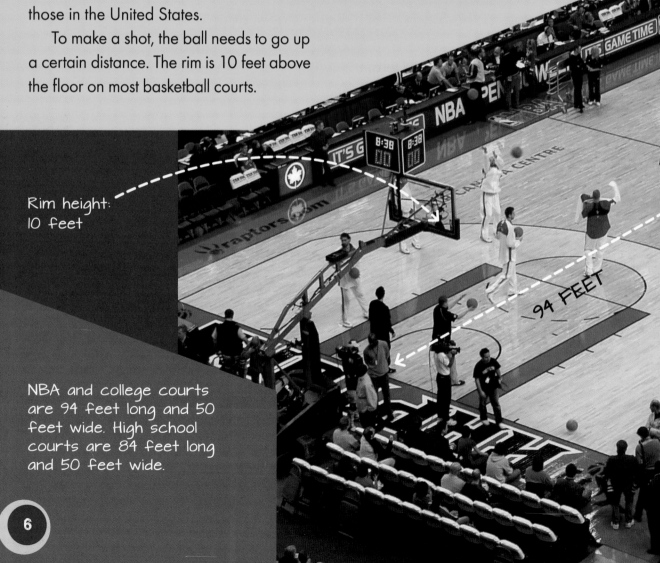

Rim height: 10 feet

94 FEET

NBA and college courts are 94 feet long and 50 feet wide. High school courts are 84 feet long and 50 feet wide.

The perimeter is the distance around the edge of the court. Add the length of the four sides to find the perimeter. A high school court's perimeter is:

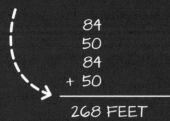

$$\begin{array}{r} 84 \\ 50 \\ 84 \\ + 50 \\ \hline 268 \text{ FEET} \end{array}$$

Area is measured in square units. Area is found by multiplying the length times the width to get square units. A high school court's area is:

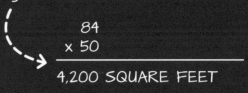

$$\begin{array}{r} 84 \\ \times 50 \\ \hline 4{,}200 \text{ SQUARE FEET} \end{array}$$

50 FEET

What about an NBA court? How much bigger is it than a high school court? Find the perimeter and area of an NBA court. Then subtract the high school totals from the NBA totals.

$$\begin{array}{r} 94 \\ 50 \\ 94 \\ + 50 \\ \hline 288 \text{ FEET} \end{array}$$

$$\begin{array}{r} 94 \\ \times 50 \\ \hline 4{,}700 \text{ SQUARE FEET} \end{array}$$

288 (NBA court) - 268 (high school court) = 20 feet

4,700 (NBA court) - 4,200 (high school court) = 500 square feet

The NBA court perimeter is 20 more feet than the high school court. The NBA court area is 500 more square feet than a high school court. NBA players are large men. They

Keeping Score

Points quickly add up to win the game. Players can earn points one, two, or three at a time. An arc at each end of the court marks the three-point line. Baskets made behind this line are three-pointers. They are the hardest to make. Free throws are worth one point. Baskets from inside the arc are worth two points.

Fouls are illegal contact by opponents. They send players to the free throw line. From there, players have time to take a 15-foot shot with no defenders. Most players make more than two out of every three free throws.

Field goals are shots taken from the court. Most pros make almost half of their two-point field goal shots. Pros make about one out of three of their three-point shots.

Shooting is measured in a **percentage**. A player who makes 3 of 8 shots has made 37.5 percent.

This percentage is found by dividing the shots made by the total shots. Then multiply the number by 100. Percent means a number out of 100.

$3 \div 8 = .375$

$.375 \times 100 = 37.5$ percent

The player who makes 3 out of 8 shots makes 37.5 out of 100.

The Denver Nuggets led the NBA in scoring during the 2011–12 season. The Nuggets hit 48 percent of their field goals. They made 33 percent of their three-pointers. They made 73 percent of their free throws.

At those rates, how many points would the Nuggets score on 100 of each shot? The field goals are worth two points each.

48 x 2 = 96 points

The three-pointers are worth three points each.

33 x 3 = 99 points

The free throws are worth one point each.

73 x 1 = 73 points

Denver Nuggets forward Danilo Gallinari (8) goes up for a shot against the Oklahoma City Thunder during a game on April 25, 2011.

Kentucky forward Anthony Davis (in white) tries to shoot against Kansas guard Tyshawn Taylor (10) during the NCAA Final Four on April 2, 2012.

How They Score

Teams that run a lot score more on fast breaks. This happens when one team hurries the ball upcourt before the **defense** has a chance to set up. Physically strong teams score close to the basket. Teams that play tough defense score after taking the ball away from the other team.

There are many ways to set up scoring chances. Coaches and people who study statistics look at the points in a game. They do this to show where each team has strength. These statistics can be very useful.

Coaches watch how points are scored during the game. They also watch videos of the game. Then they add up the points.

Coaches look at the:

- Second-chance points: how often teams score after getting offensive **rebounds**
- Points in the paint: scoring from the area between the foul line and basket
- Bench points: points by players who started the game on the bench
- Fast-break points: how well teams score in the change from defense to **offense**
- Points off **turnovers**: scoring after taking the ball away

The University of Kentucky defeated Kansas University, 67–59, in the 2012 NCAA Division I men's championship game. The ability to score off turnovers helped in the win.

KENTUCKY	CATEGORY	KANSAS
16	Points off turnovers	9
22	Points in the paint	32
2	Fast-break points	4
7	Second-chance points	6
5	Bench points	0

What percentage of Kentucky's points came off turnovers? Divide the points off turnovers by the total points.

16 (points off turnovers) ÷ 67 (total points) = .24
.24 x 100 = 24 percent

How about Kansas from the paint? Kansas's points in the paint were 32.

32 (points in the paint) ÷ 59 (total points) = .54
.54 x 100 = 54 percent

Individual Statistics

Chris Paul of the Los Angeles Clippers can fill up a **box score**. That is a score sheet that shows what happened in the game. When the game is over, Paul tends to have numbers in each of the columns listed on a box score.

Basketball players are ranked by points. They are also ranked by rebounds, **assists**, **steals**, and blocked shots. Those items are measured by **average** per game. Shooting is measured by percentage. Some players are known for scoring points. Others are known for grabbing rebounds. Still others are known for assists on baskets by teammates. Players like Paul are known for a bit of everything.

Paul played 11 games during the 2012 NBA Playoffs. His totals were:

Points	194
Rebounds	56
Assists	87
Steals	30
Blocked Shots	1
Field Goals	70-for-164
Three-pointers	13-for-39
Free Throws	41-for-47

To figure an average, divide the total points by the number of games played. Paul's averages can be found from the totals in the chart.

What is Paul's scoring average? Divide his total points by the number of games played to find out.

194 (total points) ÷ 11 (games) = 17.6
Paul's scoring average is 17.6 points per game.

You can find Paul's average in rebounds, assists, steals, and blocked shots, too. Divide each total by the number of games (11). Paul averages 5.1 rebounds, 7.9 assists, 2.7 steals, and 0.1 blocked shots.

Shooting percentages are found by dividing the made shots by the attempts. Find Paul's field goal percentage.

70 (made shots) ÷ 164 (attempts) = .427
.427 x 100 = 42.7 percent

Paul made 42.7 percent of his field goals. His three-point percentage is 33.3. His free throw percentage is 87.2.

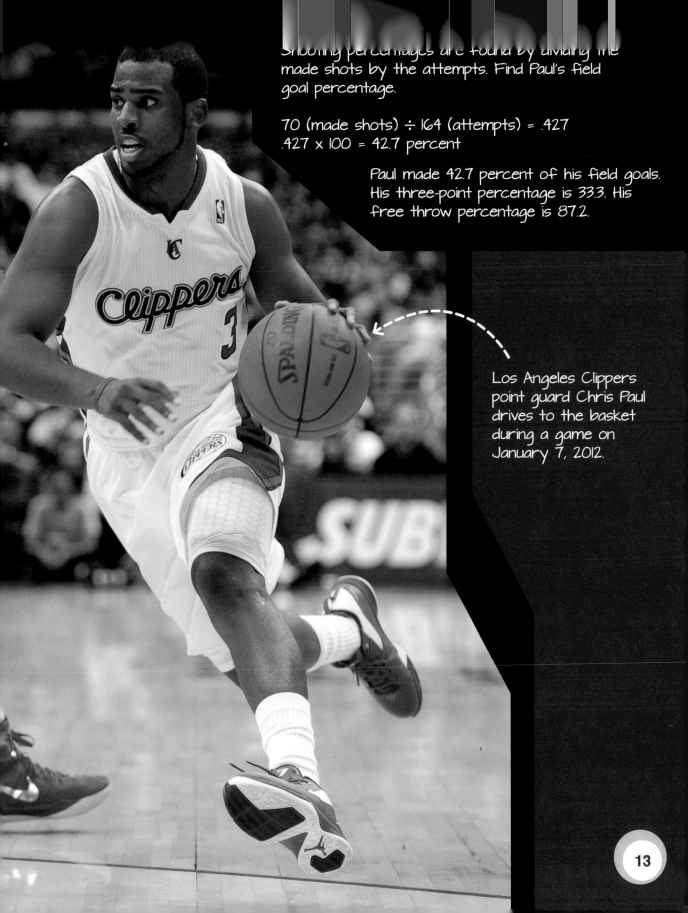

Los Angeles Clippers point guard Chris Paul drives to the basket during a game on January 7, 2012.

LeBron James (6) scores a basket during a game on February 16, 2011.

No Average Player

Some players have a way of standing out. LeBron James's physical power is clear. And all parts of his game are well above average. His many talents helped make James the Most Valuable Player in the NBA again during the 2011–12 season.

Here is how James compared to a typical NBA starter in 2011–12:

CATEGORY	LeBRON JAMES	TYPICAL NBA STARTER
Points per game	27.1	13.6
Rebounds per game	7.9	5.7
Assists per game	6.2	3.1
Steals per game	1.9	1.0
Field goal percentage	53.1	50.2

The difference between James and a typical starter can be shown in many ways. Ratios compare one number to another. The ratio of points by James to a typical player is 27.1:13.6.

Ratios can be converted to unit rates. In a unit rate, the second number in the ratio is 1. If you have a ratio of 4:2, divide the numbers by 2 to get the unit rate. The unit rate would be 2:1.

It is simple to find the unit rate for steals. The number 1 is there as a starting point. James had a ratio of 1.9:1. This is also the unit rate.

Divide 27.1 by 13.6 to find James's scoring unit rate. James comes in just under 2:1. He scored almost two points for every point made by a typical NBA starter.

The ratio of James to typical starter in rebounds is 7.9:5.7.
7.9 ÷ 5.7 = 1.39

Round that to a unit rate of 1.4:1.

Career Path

Shaquille O'Neal climbed to the top in a hurry. O'Neal averaged 23.4 points per game as a **rookie**. He was near his peak in his second season. O'Neal remained a big scorer for 12 more seasons.

In 19 seasons, O'Neal played for six teams. O'Neal finished with 28,596 points. That is the sixth-highest total in NBA history.

He played in 1,207 regular-season games. He averaged 23.7 points per game.

A line graph can show how data changes over time. When creating a line graph, first choose a title. Then label each side to explain what it shows. Choose a range of values. The range should be able to include all values.

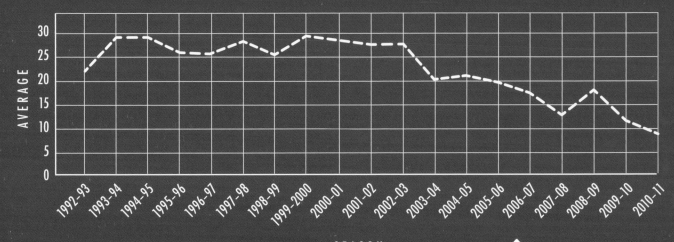

SHAQUILLE O'NEAL'S YEARLY SCORING AVERAGES

During which seasons did O'Neal's scoring average rise? Which was the longest stretch that his scoring average fell?

The line graph shows O'Neal's scoring average. It went up during the 1993-94, 1997-98, 1999-2000, 2004-05, and 2008-09 seasons. It went down two straight seasons from 2000-01 to 2001-02.

Shaquille O'Neal plays for the Miami Heat during a game on Novermber 21, 2007.

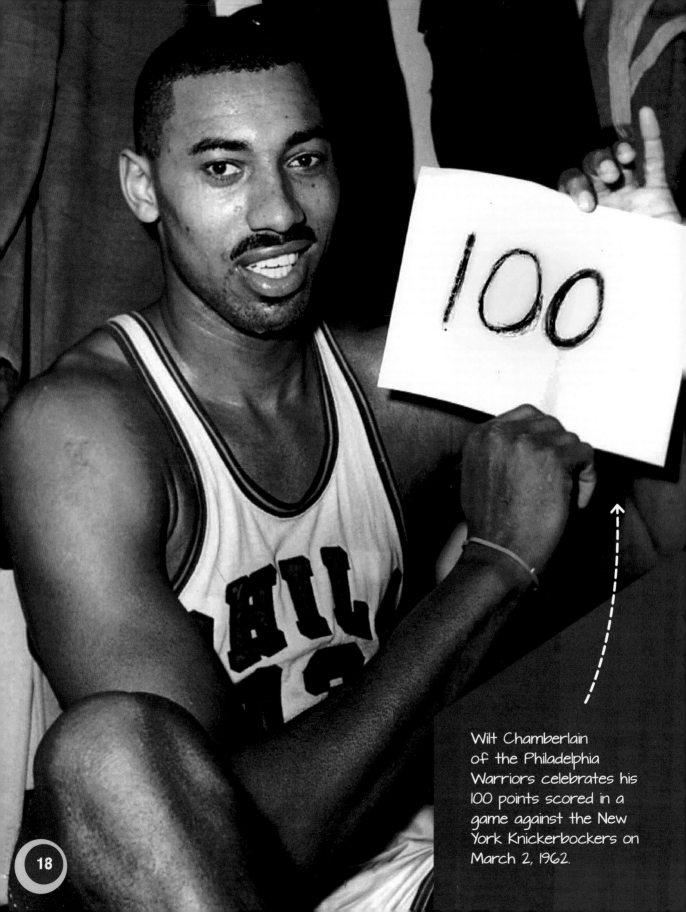

Wilt Chamberlain of the Philadelphia Warriors celebrates his 100 points scored in a game against the New York Knickerbockers on March 2, 1962.

Greatest Game Ever

It's hard for NBA teams to score 100 points in a game. The defense makes shots tough. But Wilt Chamberlain once scored 100 points all by himself.

In this game, Chamberlain started with 23 points in the first quarter. He had 18 in the second. He scored 28 in the third quarter. Then, he poured in 31 in the fourth.

The 100-point night was part of an amazing season in which Chamberlain scored more than 4,000 points. He had a record average of 50.4 points per game.

On average, Chamberlain took 40 field-goal attempts per game. And he took 17 free throws per game that season. He made 50.6 percent of his field-goal attempts. He also made 61.3 percent of his free throws.

Chamberlain's big game was on March 2, 1962. He was playing for the Philadelphia Warriors in a 169-147 win over the New York Knicks.

Chamberlain made 36 of his 63 field-goal attempts in that game.

$$36 \div 63 = 0.57$$
$$0.57 \times 100 = 57 \text{ percent}$$

Chamberlain made 57 percent of his field goals.

Chamberlain hit 28 of his 32 free throw attempts in that game.

$$28 \div 32 = 0.88$$
$$0.88 \times 100 = 88 \text{ percent}$$

Chamberlain made 88 percent of his free throws.

Zone Concepts

Coaches can have their teams defend players, areas of the floor, or both. The two most common defenses are man-to-man and **zone**. In man-to-man, each player is assigned to guard one player from the other team. In zone, each player is assigned to guard an area of the court.

The two defenses can be combined. An example is a "box-and-one" defense. In box-and-one, one defender follows a key offensive player while the other four defenders form a zone. The zone would look like a box if lines connected the players. The coach must choose between a zone and a box-and-one. He uses math to help make his decision. He wants to know how much space each defender has to cover in a box-and-one.

The coach decides what area he wants defended. It is a rectangle that is 20 feet to each side of the basket. It is 20 feet out from the backboard.

Penn State's Talor Battle (12) is guarded by Evan Turner (21) in a game against Ohio State on February 24, 2010.

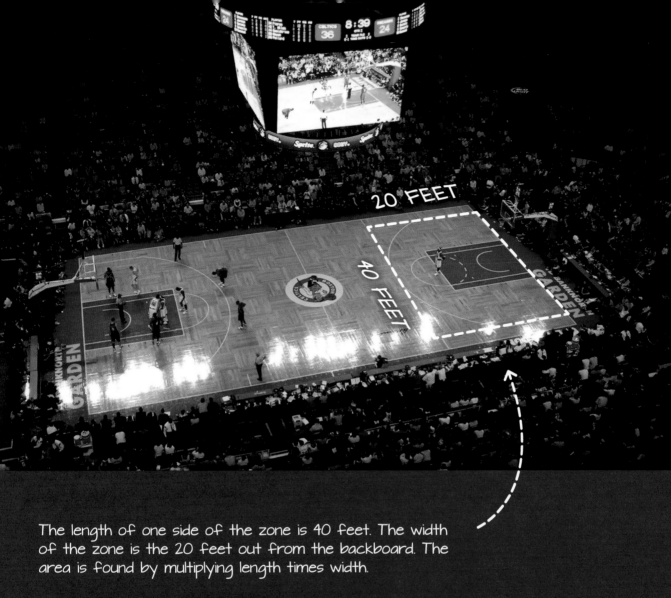

The length of one side of the zone is 40 feet. The width of the zone is the 20 feet out from the backboard. The area is found by multiplying length times width.

40 x 20 = 800
The area of the zone is 800 square feet.

Divide the area by the number of players. You will find how many square feet each player must defend.

DEFENSE	SPACE	SQUARE FEET PER PLAYER
Five-man zone	800 square feet	800 ÷ 5 = 160 square feet
Box-and-one	800 square feet	800 ÷ 4 = 200 square feet

Long Seasons

At higher levels, the games and seasons get longer. College teams play 1,200 minutes for every 800 high school minutes. That is a ratio of 1,200:800. It can be simplified to 3:2. Both numbers are divided by 400. This is the largest number that both numbers can be divided by. It reduces the ratio to its unit rate.

$$1200 \div 400 = 3$$
$$800 \div 400 = 2$$
The unit rate is 3:2.